rolling through time

rolling through time

Poems by
Dinh Le Doan

Wet Ink Books

First Edition

 Wet Ink Books
www.WetInkBooks.com
WetInkBooks@gmail.com

rolling through time
by Dinh Le Doan

Cover Design – Richard M. Grove
Layout and Design – Richard M. Grove
Cover Photograph – Richard M. Grove

Typeset in Garamond
Printed and bound in Canada
Distributed in USA by Ingram,
    – to set up an account – 1-800-937-0152

Library and Archives Canada Cataloguing in Publication

Title: Rolling through time / poems by Dinh Le Doan.
Names: Doan, Dinh Le, author.
Description: First edition.
Identifiers: Canadiana 20240381769 | ISBN 9781998324101 (softcover)
Subjects: LCGFT: Poetry.
Classification: LCC PS8607.O213 R65 2024 | DDC C811/.6—dc23

This book is dedicated to
my wife Phung,
who has encouraged
and supported me
in this endeavour.

Contents

A Book That Rolls Through Time:

An introduction to: *rolling through time*

Life is a train. Blaine Marchand

Dear readers,

I have been writing comments, blurbs, reviews, essays and book intros for Canadian poets and prose writers practically nonstop since 2017. More than a hundred fine authors have honoured my pen with their literary work. Today, I find great satisfaction in introducing an all-encompassing book by poet Dinh Le Doan, *rolling through time*.

I use the word *all-encompassing* intentionally. With his seventy poems, Le approaches, contemplates and limns a cosmic thematic territory that is remarkable, which tells of his broadband discernment in picking motifs to write about. I have oftentimes referred to Canadian poets' perceptive virtue to take in the universe around them, either within national borders or beyond, with a keen, aesthetic-cognitive eye. Le Doan is amongst them. He travels (around and into him own self), sees, construes and depicts, and we marvel at his capacity to do so.

There is plenitude of emotions, feelings, ideas crossing and re-crossing the poet's dynamic, insightful mind in the book I am presenting. As a poet, he reaches out—with hand, heart, talent—and ably, creatively touches what has called his attention. We are witnesses to a shower of recreations of reality, of life in its many-sided manifestations that are moulded by Le's penmanship.

There is, in my opinion, no better way to introduce and promote a book of poetry than by noting and exemplifying some of the poet's achievements and style through his poems. Thus, I start by saying that I am amazed by his appreciation of nature, for example, a theme he treats profusely in the book. This is an undoubtedly Canadian signature originating in the pioneer poets, who were impressed by their nation's splendor and season cycles. Read Le's "Through a Dark Autumn":

> *"Near the far edge of the bright*
> *summer dark autumn began*
> *but hid well its dark intentions*
> *beneath the rhetoric of colours…"*

Here he skillfully blends literal descriptions of the season with metaphorical detail employing personification, a useful semantic expressive means in the language. But there is much more to it while Le advances covering all four seasons with sensitive wording and *sense of change*.

Speaking of cycles, the ever-alluring notion of time, relentlessly mesmerising writers, artists, philosophers, is a recurring infatuation in the poet's conception of his oeuvre. In Le's own words, most of his pieces may be seen as *"slices of time"* reflecting the *"seasonal nature of the poems."* I daresay his "affair" with time in the book might be connected to his profession: an engineer and manager in the Canadian Space Industry. Read his poem "Time" and you will understand his passion:

> *"Time's immense. The span of each second*
> *is everywhere beyond my comprehension;*
> *and yet sitting here in my backyard with a book,*
> *it's summer, Time is nowhere.*
>   *Yet I'm not*
> *easily deceived: Time always plays nearby*
> *—I catch the resonant laughter of a child."*

He also writes about people he meets or are close or have meant a truly revealing experience to him (in "The Concert Pianist" he gives us an unforeseen, magic ending in which he fuses/reverses realities - I won't advance the ending so readers discover it directly), or about a sculpture that obviously inspired him: "Bernini's David" is a stunning piece as innovatively baroque as the painter's style. Le's artistry in his utilization of expressive means, structural arrangement, line breaks, *in crescendo* narrative, etc. is laudable:

> *"And all coiled and ready,*
> *he dwells his gaze*
> *on the advancing target as if*
> *he willed the target to loom larger*
> *before he uncoils, twirls, and fires*
> *—and thus propels his own ascension*
> *from the field of shepherds*
> *toward the realm of stars."*

From amidst his season poems, a geographical course takes him to another distant destination. "The Bay of Marea del Portillo (3)" is a reflection of the poet's fascination for regions far from his Canada:

> *"Quiet night. The tall moon plods alone*
> *along the deserted beach. A crowd*
> *of curious stars watch and sigh."*

Once more, we notice Le's inexorable nexus with time (the poem goes through three moments) and his use of personification in the phrases *"The tall moon plods alone"* and *"A crown of curious stars watch and sigh."* The poet is at ease handling these language means that acquire a stylistic status embroidering loveliness onto the lines, the poems and the book altogether.

In the overall concert of time, themes and expressive means, the poet brings in colours, sounds, sights, silhouettes, personal involvements, etc., superbly presented in "Sights and Sounds at Lake Renaud (2)":

> *"Winds are sweeping through the woods on the shore.*
> *Each tree is singing. And all together the trees sing*
> *the most cheerful songs.*
> *Voicing the footsteps of the young children running*
> *through the woods—when the day is young."*

We realize how the poet leads us through the skein of time when we read from part 1 of the poem down to part 3. I invite readers to partake in this element of sequence.

As life itself, sweet and terrible, Le takes us, on the one hand, from the beauty of nature we have been caressed by earlier to the devastation of a forest fire that "ignites" his pen and urges him to combine colours as well as direct and indirect onomatopoeia ("*roaring*" plus combinations of the sound /r/) in his description of the moment. Onomatopoeia is a powerful phonetic device in the language. In our next poem we see it in action. This is how we view nature's destructive side in "The Raging Fires of Autumn":

> "*The raging fires of autumn*
> *roaring in bright yellow*
> *orange and red atop the trees*
> *doom the leaves*
> *to a fiery death.*"

On the other hand, we are moved by his gentle, very personal piece "This, My Winter." The poem's last lines help erase from our minds the vivid images he conveyed in the previous poem:

> "*these*
> *are the graces*
> *on the mornings of this, my winter.*"

As a whole, Le Doan's book is a testimony of life, an artist's testimony—because Le *portrays* scenes and sensations—, who is quite acquainted with the world surrounding him, be it pleasant, terrible, cold, hot, mild, grey, near, or overseas. Besides, the poet explores the inner self, carving from it some of the original pieces we read here. Le embarks on a temporal journey in which he is not alone: his rendering of poetry captures our sensibility and takes us on a ride that will leave us fulfilled, curious, awed, nourished.

Enjoy Le Doan's *rolling through time*. It is a worth-reading volume, exquisitely edited and shaped into what we now have in our hands.

Le's legacy to CanLit is commendable. Let's thank him for sharing his poetry as we thank the publisher for making the charm of this book come to light. I entitled my Introduction rephrasing Le's line from his opening poem "Through a Dark Autumn," "… *the train / that rolls through time,*" deliberately again, because this is Le's contribution to life and literature. It is like a train (as my quotation from Marchand tells us in respect to life) that will never stop, either in time or in space. And this line reminds me of an icon, Shakespeare, whose Sonnet XVIII tempts me to quote from: "*When in eternal lines to time thou grow'st, / So long as men can breathe, or eyes can see, / So long lives this, and this gives life to thee.*" As long as poetry is there, poets shall live; as long as there are poets, poetry shall endure. Le joins the group of those who leave "*eternal lines*" for us.

Allow me to close by citing a distinguished Canadian scholar, poet, lit essayist and editor, James Deahl: "… *the poetry being written today in Canada is as important, and as varied, as any other English-language poetry.*" (Taken from *Tamaracks: Canadian Poetry for the 21st Century*, Lummox Press, 2018). Le Doan honours this statement: his poetry is significant, for it qualitatively preserves for the future his vision of the world; and it is varied, for it looks at and turns into valuable, wide-ranging poetic illumination both the themes he resorts to and the forms he visits and revisits in his writing.

Read Dinh Le Doan's *rolling through time*. You will thank me later for the invitation and will certainly thank Le for his book. *Time* will tell.

Associate Professor Miguel Ángel Olivé Iglesias

Through a Dark Autumn

Near the far edge of the bright
summer dark autumn began
but hid well its dark intentions
beneath the rhetoric of colours. Shades of

overripe yellow and flashes
of bombastic red started to appear
on the summer's landscape. Stealthily at first.
Then more showed up and spread out

to smother the summer's green. Leaves began
to die. Trees bared their murky souls.
The air turned cold. Birds fled for their lives.
And wagon trains in dark grey

hovered in the sky and dumped
load after load of sleet onto the world.
Darkness grew. The sun woke up
fumbling in the dark.

And dark autumn brings
more darkness as we journey through
like the picture windows of the train
that rolls through time.

Stories Heard at the Lake

The lake's sleeping in the dark.
But its sleep's woefully disturbed.
Geese have descended. How did they find
the lake in the faint starlight?

Yet their harsh voices shatter the stillness
as they talk. Or tell their stories. Stories
of the hazards they encountered. Stories
about those whom they knew who are now absent.
Stories of a species of migrants.

And in the morning, trees converse
in bright autumn colours along the shore.
Maples and birches talk and conifers whisper
to the young trees the old tales

passed down through generations
of the times when their ancestors migrated here
in ancient ships which rode
the currents of the air. None was a native and yet
they stood guard for this shore.

Toddlers

Toddlers are the stars
of the playground. Wherever they go
their caregivers follow and circle around.

As if tethered to them by
binding forces of attraction.

And like the roaming stars, toddlers
constantly toddle or run.

Or rock back and forth on the constellation
of spring riders.

Or climb up the stairs toward the heavens before
shooting down the slides.

And shine and twinkle in their dazzling displays.
And climb up again as if

circulating and pulsating inside each of them
were the unbounded energy
of a burgeoning star.

Bernini's David

His eyes narrow, his jaws clench,
and his muscular arms and shoulders twist
against the powerful hips
in the coiled position he has practiced
thousands of times before
in the shepherds' field.
And the round stone in his sling awaits
forceful release
to deliver the killing blow.
And all coiled and ready,
he dwells his gaze
on the advancing target as if
he willed the target to loom larger
before he uncoils, twirls, and fires
—and thus propels his own ascension
from the field of shepherds
toward the realm of stars.

Outside Inside

Outside, the rock-lined bank of the Danube
tries hard to touch the low water
of the river with its feet.

Trees can speak without their murmur.
Some shout in loud yellow colours
hollering autumn to the other shore.

And the setting sun lays its soft
orange fingers on the face of an old building
above the river's lock.

The building looks happy:
I am rooted here but I have survived
two great wars.

Water continues its glimmering
conversation with the sky until twilight.
The day's job is done.

It heads down into the cruise ship's lounge
which has turned on the lights.

It relaxes and stretches out inside,
nursing a glass of hot wine.

Piano music makes its head swing
from side to side.

A peaceful moment to enjoy.
Peace is local and fragile.

The Bay of Marea del Portillo

1
Calm daybreak. Wrinkly water. Slender waves
roll over in their silvery furs before
splaying flat on the shore.

2
Hot midday. Two gigantic green
elephants cooling themselves in the bay's
blue water where mountains meet the sea.

3
Quiet night. The tall moon plods alone
along the deserted beach. A crowd
of curious stars watch and sigh.

Large Snowflakes Burst Out

Large snowflakes burst out
of the laden sky and drop down
profusely in open parachutes.

Snowflakes land upon
the cragged bare arms of trees
and the fully clothed darker pines.

And entomb the roofs of houses in white.
The land's conquered and muted.
It stops being

its old self for a while. There's not
a breath of wind. And the hot sun's
nowhere to be seen.

A gleaming snowy landscape encased in
a large glass bell jar glazed
with a wintry shade of grey.

Snow Is Falling

Snow is falling. The earth turns white.
Its new skin is as smooth as silk.
The sun hides behind a veil.

I stay confined inside my shelter
while the cedars run between the houses
and collect snowflakes outside.

Running past my window the cedars see
a bear-like creature inside a cave
immersed in dreams.

None sees me. I am the dreams.

Early May at the Lake

The sly old winter staged its comeback.
The sharp-eyed groundhog saw
its shadow being stretched some more.

Leaves stay indoors. Trees wear no clothes—
having spent all
their hard-earned wages on the frivolous snow.

And yet floating ice,
in large patches of rich blue-silver and white,
still resides on the lake.

Only plain water migrates.

A most gutsy climb over the border wall,
and yet reaching only
a swampy slum on the other side.

The Concert Pianist

Through her half-open window, she lets out
a series of sweet notes, the melodious raindrops,
repeats and repeats till a lively
mountain stream comes to life
in the opening of the concerto
she has chosen to practice this afternoon.

The fast notes flow down to the sidewalk
like a small stream emptying into a pond.
And although the rhythm and cadence appear
natural, they follow a pre-composed order
and flow downwards, like all her years
wholly dedicated to daily practice
that have come and to come.

The flows of orderly movements
and the confident strikes
her agile fingers are raining on the keyboard
give her the illusion of control, yet that
which she so loves,
unbeknown to her, takes over control of her life.

Violent Winds Hit the Lake Hard

Violent winds hit the lake hard. All day.
Trees sway drunkenly.
Birds hang up their wings.

And a large crowd of indifferent clouds
jostling one another to gawk at
angry winds and waves bullying

the trembling boat docks
whose stiff fingers are gripping
onto the shore and don't let go.

Unsettled. The lake grimaces
as it watches.
When will calm water

and sunshine return? When will
its watchful eye behold
a better world?

Sunrise on the Lake

The sky turns pinkish. A crow proudly
spreads out its wings and hovers in the air.
And caws loudly. Taunting eternity.
Only the living

can awaken at dawn. And the sun polishes
the lake's surface to a mirror finish
hiding a dark world beneath
where long-dead trees

which had once spread out their wings
as proudly on this shore
now lie motionless, their bones scoured clean,
in the murky water. Unaware.

And a loon dives deep. Connecting the two worlds.
From the dark a fish surfaces
trading a few perfect
circles for a gulp of air.

Cloudburst Above the Lake

I
Drops of water are returning to the lake in large numbers.
Armies of them on invisible parachutes.

Success for each drop means
falling back to the lake with a decent splash

creating enlarging circles of impact before dissolving.
And each drop has only one chance to do this well.

II
The complacent kayakers are caught surprised
by the thirty-per-cent-chance rain becoming real. They mutter
under their soured breaths, "Who voted for this?!"

And the ducks give up their dabbling at the lily patch
to shelter under a birch tree. "What?! What?! What?"
—What's good about this hard-hitting rain?!

The birch bends down as if to answer. But "What? What?
What?"
—The ducks can't make out the answer under the heavy
downpour.

The World of the
Mirror Lake at Night

The rows of trees on the opposite shore turn into
a dark castle wall in which the darker houses hide
their dark and hard faces.

A lonesome star comes down and kisses a tree
heeding the tremolos of frog calls
resounding along the shore.

And a car sweeps its light beams around the curve.
Looking for answers. But true answers lie
in the dark and shaky world below the waterline.

And a goose rushes across the lake and lets out a cry.
As if trying to rescue someone
who's drowning in the truth they fail to see.

Night and Day

It's Night.
Darkness overwhelms the world.
But there are
some promising lights.

The lone streetlight upon the hill
tries hard to be the moon. And
the distant stars, however faint,
are striving to shine.

Then in the late Night sky begins
a pale blue light
glowing faintly at first above
the horizon then grows brighter
moment-by-moment.

The lake lets the lights in
but menacing dark figures still lurk
in the murky water where big boulders
and downed trees lie until

the whole sky brightens.
A burning white disk appears
in the eye of the red house
on the opposite shore. It's Day.

A Jet Plane Flies Past

A jet plane flies past screaming. Yet not
one bird flies past and screams
at the oppressive summer heat
as if the birds knew
summer days are fleeting.

White clouds remain calm. They lounge
leisurely in the sky and have
no mind to gather and no qualms about
procrastinating, as if they owned time.

In the persistent dryness, shoreline
greenery feels itchy in the throat.
It's desperate for a drink like the circling
bald eagle that's desperate for a meal.

And on the lake's surface, a swarm of
insects obsessed with the limelight
are scurrying madly toward the place
where thousands of stars sparkle.

The Sky's Laden

The sky's laden
with heavy anxiousness.
Birds stop singing.

Then booms a loud thunder.
Thunder after thunder. Like shots
from giant cannons.

Then the heavens open and dump
torrents of water onto the lake.
Dropping rock hard liquid

on the cottage roof.
Fearful tears running down the windowpanes.
Then suddenly the rain stops.

Red roses lose their fragile petals.
Yet wet leaves glitter. And blue sky
and white clouds return
to the lake's water.

Trees:

All that they become, after their leaf sprouting
days are over, are downed bodies of trees;
yet here on the forest's floor they lie returning:

their splintered trunks and limbs serve as places
of refuge; their former days in the sun now scent
the morning air; and out of the decaying skins,
clusters of mushrooms and green shoots grow;

and above them cries a watchful crow: its
sharp caw resonates in the air, acclaiming that
the downed remains give rise to some things new.

Lake Renaud in November

The lake is a large plain of snow and ice.
Boat docks lose their life's purpose.
What can they do but go to sleep?
And soundly they sleep under white blankets.

The sky blows chilly breaths. Vigilant cottages
keeping watch along the shore
send smoke signals to warn the city
that winter will arrive early.

Snow covers the bald spots of nearby hills.
Like whipped cream. Rocks protrude
like embedded chocolate. Festive
cream cakes that celebrate the Earth.

The Earth Tilts Its Head Back

The earth tilts its head back further
and the slanting sun becomes
a glob of flame that loses its warmth.
Midwinter.

We live in a chilly world.
Trees clatter their teeth on bad wind days.
And snow raining down
day after day. The earth's belly swells

with undigested snow.
And the cedar hedge blooms white
from head to toe. And on a rare
warm day ice may fall

from the sky. Icy remains
of a wayward comet that plunged to earth
—lest we think the worst's over
in midwinter.

Sights and Sounds at Lake Renaud

1
The trees and bushes on this shore and on
the opposite shore are green. So are their reflections.
And the leaves of the water lilies that thrive
on the lake are green.

And amidst all this green from shore to shore
a red canoe rests—a red dash placed
for special emphasis in the midst
of a green poem.

2
Winds are sweeping through the woods on the shore.
Each tree is singing. And all together the trees sing
the most cheerful songs.

Voicing the footsteps of the young children running
through the woods—when the day is young.

3
Yet the songs turn sombre late in the day—
when the day takes on
the colours of the setting sun.

A Summer Day at the Cottage

A branch waves lightly greeting the dawn.
But the early morning call of a blue jay resounds—
the sour notes break through the stillness and stick
briefly to the air then fall off.

The rare grey heron lands on the lake early
and treads the warm water
in a watchful manner but still does not stay long.
For fear of being seen and harassed.

The fiery midday sun divides
the shaded sundeck into a cool zone and a hot zone
separating the fortunate from the unfortunate.

The tied kayak keeps banging its shoulder
against the old cottage dock—seeking release.
Wanting its freedom back.

But the old dock remains unyielding.
Like someone who has lost his senses
and becomes dogmatic.

The setting sun keeps itself awake long
in the evening, longing to see again
the beloved stars it has sorely missed.

The Sky Is Full of Shining Stars

The sky is full of shining stars.
Most are shining brightly yet some
are burning out as we speak.
And one, perhaps amongst
the most ancient of all the stars,
will soon perish.
It's hard to predict
which one. Yet when a star dies,
it outshines all the others
and thus catches our eyes.

See how bright it shines in its last moment.
As if it wanted us to take notice
of its gesture of final farewell.
And even though we know
that such an event will occur once in a while
in the heavens full of stars,
when we catch sight of one that shines
for the last time,
something ancient within us stirs
—awakens and shines in return.

The Raging Fires of Autumn

The raging fires of autumn
roaring in bright yellow
orange and red atop the trees
doom the leaves
to a fiery death.

No autumn rain can douse the fires.
They thus keep on burning until
they burn themselves out

and leave behind
lonesome bare trees standing
over a large field
of burned out bodies of the leaves.

Field after field.
Vast as an ocean.

October Light

Bright sunlight dazzles the leaves
outside my bedroom window.

A more sober version descends
on my clock radio

upon which an errant light ray
tumbles and scatters.

And yet "No matter," it says.
"A light ray moves on

without any burden," it says
as it lands on me on this October day.

Landscape of Abandonment

Trees have abandoned
their hard-working leaves to the cruel
November winds. The winds pluck the leaves off

one by one. And cold nights let frost
descend upon the shore. The wild
flowers that thrived here

are here no more. And a layer of ice newly formed
on the lake shuts tight
the food cupboard's door

upon the birds. Migrating birds stop
dropping by the lake when it closes
its heart and door.

White November

November gallops to flee
this wintry city
but its hind legs get caught
in the chill white mud.

And the shivering oak tree
hoists high its tattered sail
in a last-ditch
effort to sail south.

But hardy houses brave the chill.
They hunker down and don
white knit caps
to keep themselves warm.

This, My Winter

White,
fluffy,
fresh snow
on the brown cedars
outside my kitchen window;

green,
steamy,
your hot cup of tea
warming my hands;

luminous,
smooth,
pale-white skin,
your neck and shoulders;

these
are the graces
on the mornings of
this, my winter.

Winter Morning at the Lake

Morning playfully climbs down the trees
of the opposite western shore.
Houses flash their eyes.
Metal chimneys glitter.

Then Morning grows taller.
It now stands tall against
a gigantic blue vault, looks down
and challenges all to measure up.

An intrepid little bird heeds the call,
beats its wings vigorously
and crosses the large and deep divide
between two tall trees.

And the brave tree shadows
crawl en masse across the vast field of snow
to reach the sunnier shore.
A few succeed.

Out Here in the Cottage Country

Out here in the cottage country darkness is king.
But not tonight. Tonight the moon is out casting
a downward gaze on the rear
viewing deck, and a dreamy blue light
over the black-and-white landscape

of gleaming snow-covered lake with trees
crowding the shoreline. Still, one can make out
the heads of the tall pines which stand
absorbed in a dream. They dream to roam.
They dream freedom.

Snowy Winter: Old and Young

The sky is an old man.
Its hairs are all grey.

But the land is much older—
a lot more white than grey.

Living in this unchanging white
and grey, the day
soon forgets its name.

And under heavy white helmets
overburdened old houses
feel their age.

Only the energetic snow blower has
the best time of its life

gobbling up snow and blowing
snow plumes into the air.

Sunrise at Marea del Portillo

Darkness still covers the shore
and surrounding Maestra mountains
when the sun begins to rise

and colour the sky blue
the gathering clouds grey
the calm surface of the bay silver

and parts of the sky and clouds
luminous orange.

Then the sun smiles roundly
at its completed colouring work
to turn night into day.

Trees in the Winter

Trees in the winter stand forlorn
and look greyer
than the grey sky against which they stand.

And they appear half dead as though
they have withdrawn
from life and now live within

the sweet memories of their springs and summers
which were etched deep
within their cores.

The Beauty of Winter

The cottage does not take its eyes off
the pristine whiteness of the frozen lake
wholly covered
by a thick layer of snow

and the fluffy whiteness that decorates
the dark pine trees and the bare
brownish boughs

and the playful whiteness of each flake
of falling snow
falling in an unhurried way

to take in fully
the beauty of winter
the beauty of the colours that are here

and of the colours that do not show
of the white light's
hidden rainbow.

A Pink Glow

A pink glow begins to show
above the rows of trees.
Early morning.

But does this make a difference
to the obstinate frozen lake
fixed in its ways beneath
a thick layer of snow?

Grey smoke from the cottage's chimney
rises toward the drifting clouds as though
wanting to join a similar crowd and drift
with the flow
so it doesn't have to think.

Whereas the tall pine tree
in the corner of the rear yard
stands alone for the sake of independent thinking.
Not mindlessly re-whispering
the truths or the untruths.

And the warm water world
appears vividly in the early morning dreams
of the kayaks and the canoes
hibernating along the shore.

On This First Warm Day

On this first warm day of March
snow still sits on the rooftops
staircases and sidewalks of Montreal.
Yet a new warmth arrives
with the bright sunlight.

And the sweet smell of fresh
water vapour fills the air.
And under the roofs
of grey-stone dwellings
the house sparrows sing aloud—

the warm sun returns and shines
inside each of them.

Spring Rain

Trees and bushes in bare forms are reaching up
beyond their earthly confines. They're on a new
fulfilling journey.

The supporting ground rises up from its long
frozen position to welcome the rain:
I haven't seen you for a long time.

The clear-eyed window brushes away
the hindering raindrops that crawl
on its eyes like insects.

Cosmic Carousel

The hedge and trees are in the dark yet
the sky's a light grey into which imbues
a subtle light—night turns

steadily into day. And in the valleys of rooftops
the old winter snow turns pale white
and hides from

the hunting spring wielding a deadly scythe.
And yet winter simply morphs into spring.
There's no end or

beginning on the cosmic carousel. The flying
ponies continue to fly
non-stop their playful rounds.

Peace on the Rhine

The cruise ship moves slowly
like the passage of leisure time
on the Rhine in late March.

All along the river's banks
the houses look neat and orderly.
The junks must hide nearby.

And each town that the ship passes by
boasts a towering church
lording it over the houses.

Yet the rocky hills and sloping vineyards.
already green, chose to live outside
the towns and cities to avoid

war's damages, and atrocities.
The lazing white swans on the water
are spared. They are not

on history's menus. Still, some fearless birds
dive-bomb the Rhine out of habit.
But now is peacetime.

Peace on the Rhine, however impermanent,
has given them and us
more lucrative opportunities.

Kayaking in May

Bright colours have returned
to the lake and surrounding hills.
Trees prefer light green colours
but some choose reddish brown.

And silence returns to the lake
when the loon stops wailing. Or when
I can hear my kayak say
"A bit to the left." And then

"A bit to the right." I listen
and strive to balance both sides
to glide forward—and let
city life trail behind.

In My Dream

In my dream we meet: I stand waiting, and
about to speak when you hurry away
to Baxter College.
                              We never meet face-
to-face, as if by being near we can
throw hurts at each other. Who takes the blames
for making us lose? Who was the last to play?
Who lost the game? Our debts cry to be paid.
Would talking be enough to own the peace again?

Where was love hidden in the prizes we had
won from years of trophy hunting—the game
being played? When, to look for it, I stopped visiting,
you could call, but no; you played marriage instead,
in a rush. Where was love?
                              When we meet again,
I'll stop to speak to you—in my dream.

Watching the Sunset on Bar Harbor

Our feeling has followed the sun's
downward path toward the water
long before we begin to notice:
it has been out with the sun and jointly descending,
and is now gleaming and rippling on the inlet.
But what causes the feeling to ripple?

Perhaps it is disturbed by the notion
that all which it beholds and holds dear,
like the sunlit inlet and surrounding hills
and the sailing vessels that anchor here,
will soon disappear
in the unrelenting rising darkness,
which is all encompassing.

The Green Gift

Outside the bay window
tall maples, poplars, and ashes
in bulging green coats and hats
cover most of the grey sky.

Still, there's enough sunlight
getting through in the long day
to make the leaves happy.
Leaves are dancing in the breeze.

And flotillas of daylilies, having arrived
in the large green bay outside,
with tall sailing masts

rigged with green flower buds above
the long oars of green linear leaves,
now row into the summer.

And the street that runs through the neighbourhood
is a silky grey ribbon
that ties the green gift

which is bestowed upon us
after a long white winter
and a rainy spring.

All That Green

All that green that lives in my backyard
grows into a darker green in July:

Now the tall hedge becomes
a dark wall of greedy cedars
which devour the lives of the sunlight
that strays onto them.

Perhaps, as the cedars grow,
they learn enough to know
about the short growing season,
and about yesterday, today, and tomorrow.

Perhaps they know what we know
yet all the while feel
more content and secure
in their ever greenness.

The Sun Lifts Up

The sun lifts up
the dark curtain draping
over the lake.

Tall green sentries emerge
from darkness standing guard
over their beloved shore.

The sky holds its breath.
White clouds float freely
in the blue water as in the air.

And white lily flowers open wide
and decorate the cove.
An early arrival duck is flying low

and lands on a runway
paved with green lily leaves.
A quiet green airport
begins its day.

Shades of Green

Shades of green are the colours of my walks.
Brighter green are the young leaves in the early spring.
Darker green are the maturing leaves now in June.
Blended green is the faithful tracksuit which
you bought and mended with mixed green stitches
over several decades, which I wear.

Stars Over Lake O'Neal

Countless stars are shining
in the dark
night sky over the lake.
Yet however bright
or dim each star shines
they shine
in profound loneliness.
The dark and vast chasm
that lies between two stars
cannot be bridged.
And thus laden with pain
the stars send
their constant throbbing
into our world and beyond.

The Shared Path

On this sun-soaked peninsula I walk
the dirt path that points ahead, yet goes
to nowhere but a dead end — from there one
could watch the sun go down with its last rays.

I walk alone yet I'm not alone out here:
a white crane returns to its family and home
on the tree, and a blue heron treads
the mangrove's water working late for its meal.

It looks like each of us is doing
a different thing, yet we have much in common:
choices to make and things to do along the path
which trains our minds ahead toward sundown.

After the Heavy Summer Rain

After the heavy summer rain
bushes and trees glisten from head to feet.
The lake's amply filled.

The cottage dock
dips its flat beak into the lake and drinks
to its heart's content. The sky

still wears a grey mask.
Outdoor table and chairs remain
slippery.

The worn out handrail of the drenched
sundeck sees
upon clear reflection

the hard truth about itself—its vision
of flying past the grey clouds is
but a midsummer's dream.

Reflection

the tree that stands
near the edge
of the pond
sees
the deep blue abyss
into which it would
one day tip
and fall
without end

In the Early Morning

In the early morning I came
unto you, my wooded sanctuary,
into your fresh, arising scents,
upon your rocks, roots, twigs and leaves,
into the streams of your dawning light,
onto your bird choir full of praises
to the early morning, another day.

Lake O'Neil in August

So calm it holds the thought
of the sky
so blue it colours blue
your brown eyes
and so quiet it lets you hear
the murmur of the trees
living on its shore.

October Blues

The sun shines brightly but the day's
in a dark mood—it has slowly turned darker
at both ends. And geese are

squawking in the sky. Fleeing the place
where they were born and raised
they lament as they fly.

And the orange and red
have taken over the green
atop the trees. Leaves see no future.

The anxious ones try to glide
away early but their poorly crafted sails
fail to catch the winds.

Autumn Leaves

Autumn leaves have been falling,
falling near and far.

So silently they fall, they make no sound
when they fall and hit the ground where
standing over them dressed in dark suits
are trees in solemn mourning
and devoid of comforting thoughts,

except perhaps the trees' own knowledge
that leaves are born in the spring
to fall before the winter to save the trees,

and that some leaves, despite their predicament,
have managed to grow and realize
their true colours,
and have lived fully thus for a time
before they fall.

Sunday Coffee

I sip your coffee
slowly
this Sunday morning
so not to spill
a single drop;

it smells aromatic
and tastes
bittersweet
as it's been
over the decades;

draws
the swirling steam
over the cup
a warm
lingering smile.

Late Autumn

A crow's flying from tree to tree
and caws loudly at each stop—
alarmed at a new cold whiteness
that grew overnight on the land.

Still, some houses keep their eyes closed.
As though refusing to see the new reality
when it doesn't match
their long-held view.

But it's only eager winter
having set its long sight upon autumn
now making a sudden appearance.
An early visit.

Yet the autumn sun
behind the morning's haze
casts its most angry look—fuming mad at losing
its powerful hot grip upon the world.

Cold Winter Morning

sunlight through the windowpane
sparkles

upon the river of ice
formed on the glass

evoking
poetic beauty

I stand motionless
in case

sunlight
sparkles upon me

Frigid December

The sun has steadily turned down its furnace.
The warm days had taken flight southward
like a flock of migrating birds.

And a large mass of frigid air from the north
a giant dragon that exhales icy breaths arrives
and circles over us. And refuses to leave.

The cold space between two houses turns
much colder. And close neighbours now live
like isolated cosmonauts.

Sketch of April

Dark as night.
Then twenty percent light.
Then more light appears
to usher in the new day.

April's snow dissolves
into the ground. Water
that rose from the earth
now returns to the earth.

Life goes full circle.
It can't be helped.

Buried grasses emerge.
Pallid and flattened.
But primed to rise and embrace
the blessed new life they have obtained.

The shingle roofs glisten in the rain.
In the ever-changing sky it is written
that change is inevitable.

Cold Spring

Pink clouds all gather at dawn
to relay a command from the arid sky
to the creative earth.

Go forth and write.

New words in bright green
begin to sprout
out of the snow-moistened ground

then climb up the trees
to fill in the blanks
on bare branches

describing spring
with utmost vibrancy.

All the anxious waiting
brought earlier
by the spell of

cold and barren spring
vanishes.

Raindrops

the sky turns dark
under thick rain clouds

the raindrops fall
upon the leaves

each drop sounds out
its distinct note

desperate to be heard
before reaching

the silent ground

As the Morning Grows

A pot of steaming hot tea
a bowl of cooked red beans
and fruits on a plate.

And the silhouettes
of the backyard's trees
form a large V sign greeting
the blue and pink
dawning sky.

I feast on them
and turn pinker
as the morning grows.

Sundown on the Lake

The sun sinks behind
the tall rows of trees
that have struggled hard to rise
above the crowded hill
upon which they started out.

And in the sky
the day vents out
its large tongues of fire
in blue, purple, and white.

Its burning rage when witnessing
the steady decline of the Light.

And on the surface of the lake
Darkness and Light play
their endgame of the day.
With passion.

Suddenly
half of the Light is gone
and Darkness wins.

Evening

The hectic day slows
to a stop.

Neighbours retreat
into their lairs.

The street breathes
a sigh of relief.

The burned out sky
closes its eye.

Darkness arrives
upon thousands

of shady steps.

Outside My Bedroom Window

Outside my bedroom window
is a shining and colourful scene.
The roofs of nearby houses are large
gleaming patches of black or brown,
the crisscrossing tree branches form
blue-tinted lines of grey,
and the clusters of young leaves,
sprouting in abundance, shine
as dashes of bright green.
May it is, the heart of spring,
posing as a large
and beautiful painting,
except for the hidden bird that sings
quick quick quick quick quick
marking May
as Time.

Time

Time's immense. The span of each second
is everywhere beyond my comprehension;
and yet sitting here in my backyard with a book,
it's summer, Time is nowhere.

                           Yet I'm not
easily deceived: Time always plays nearby
—I catch the resonant laughter of a child.

Colours of Grey

On this first day of snowfall
the snow arrives slow and wet
is seen streaking across
the green cedar hedge
extinguishes the flames of red
leaves on the neighbourhood trees
smothers their branches to a charcoal grey
imbues the fall sky with a smoky grey
dousing this fall day in the cold ashes
of bleached grey in the aftermath.

The Winter Night

The winter night
suddenly shows itself
outside my bedroom window
all white and silent
with its head hanging low
like someone
who is full of sorrow and regret
when facing loneliness.
The caressing winds
which have been here all day
have left for good.

Hope and Despair

The heavy weight of winter is lifted.
The cottage's dock and sundeck are free
to rise into spring.

New leaves are crowding
on tree branches. Trees sprout and grow
their own futures.

A creative bird lays a new flight path
over the water by overlaying
moment upon moment.

But cries a wistful loon in the distance
lamenting my ignorance
of timeless poetry.

Her Wish

In this tourist area of the Old City she sits,
through her long hours upon its sidewalk,
crafting and selling her voodoo dolls.

She crafts their bodies after her body,
their faces after her face, and infuses her
spirit into each of the dolls that she creates.

And she labours hard to sell her dolls as if
to cast her spirit more far and wide,
around the world, making her be more than
her self—As if she wished to be her art.

.

An Afterword from the Publishers,
Richard M. Grove

In *rolling through time*, poet Dinh Le Doan, embarks on a lyrical exploration of the passage of time, weaving together the thematic threads of nature, seasons, and personal reflection across seventy poems. Le's mastery of language is evident as he skillfully blends the literal and metaphorical, employing devices such as personification and onomatopoeia to enrich his vivid depictions of seasonal transitions and human experiences.

The collection opens with "Through a Dark Autumn," setting the tone with its nuanced portrayal of autumn's dual nature—visually stunning yet foreboding. This poem exemplifies Le Doan's ability to capture the essence of a moment, a recurring motif throughout the book. His engineering background, particularly his involvement in the Canadian Space Industry, subtly informs his poetic perspective, lending a unique analytical depth to his contemplation of time and space.

Le Doan's poetry is deeply rooted in Canadian literary traditions, yet it transcends geographical boundaries, reflecting universal themes of life, change, and endurance. This first collection by Le is not merely a set of poems but a journey through the cyclical nature of life, inviting readers to reflect on their own experiences of time and existence. The careful editing and selection of poems enhances the book's appeal, making it a noteworthy contribution to CanLit. It is a compelling read for anyone fascinated by the poetic interplay of nature and time.

Introduction by: Miguel Ángel Olivé Iglesias.

BEd, English Major. Associate Professor of Holguín University. He has a Master's degree in English. He has published more than thirty books as author/coauthor, editor/coeditor, literary reviewer, proofreader and translator. He is the V.P. of the Canada Caribbean Literary Alliance, the Editor-in-chief of the CCLA magazine, *The Ambassador*, and a translator for the "CanLit in Translation" Series. He has published numerous books with SandCrab Books, Hidden Brook Press, Wet Ink Books and QuodSermo Publishing.

About the Author

Dinh Le Doan (Le as he's known to his friends) was born in South Vietnam; he now lives in Beaconsfield, Québec. He has a PhD in engineering from the University of New South Wales in Sydney, Australia, and has worked since 1978 in the Canadian space industry as an engineer and manager. During his retirement he devotes his time to writing poetry in English, his second language. His visually striking, thoughtful, and compassionate poems were well received by Canadian poets and editors. His poems have appeared in *Tower Poetry*, *Montreal Sérai* and *Devour: Art & Lit Canada*. *"rolling through time"* is his first book of poems.

Email: dledoan67@gmail.com.

Acknowledgement

Through a Dark Autumn – *p. 6*
Previously published in the Winter 2021/22 Issue of Tower Poetry.

Stories Heard at the Lake – *p. 7*
Previously published in the Winter 2021/22 Issue of Devour: Art & Lit Canada.

Toddlers – *p. 8*
Previously published in the Winter 2023/24 Issue of Devour: Art & Lit Canada.

Bernini's David – *p. 9*
Previously published in Vol. 28, Issue 2 of Montréal Serai.

The Bay of Marea del Portillo – *p. 11*
Previously published in the Summer 2023 Issue of Tower Poetry.

Large Snowflakes Burst Out – *p. 12*
Previously published in the Winter 2021/22 Issue of Tower Poetry.

Snow Is Falling – *p. 13*
Previously published in Vol. 32, Issue 4 of Montréal Serai.

The Concert Pianist – *p. 15*
A variation of this poem was previously published in Vol. 28, Issue 2 of Montréal Serai.

Violent Winds Hit the Lake Hard – *p. 16*
Previously published in the Winter 2023/24 Issue of Tower Poetry.

Sunrise on the Lake – *p. 17*
A variation of this poem was previously published in the Summer 2020 Issue of Devour: Art & Lit Canada.

Cloudburst Above the Lake – *p. 18*
Previously published in Vol. 31, Issue 4 of Montréal Serai.

The World of the Mirror Lake at Night – *p. 19*
Previously published in the Winter 2019/20 Issue of Tower Poetry.

A Jet Plane Flies Past – *p. 21*
Previously published in the Summer 2023 Issue of Devour: Art & Lit Canada.

Trees: - *p. 23*
Previously published in the Winter 2012/13 Issue of Tower Poetry.

Lake Renaud in November – *p. 24*
Previously published in the Summer 2021 Issue of Tower Poetry.

The Earth Tilts Its Head Back – *p. 25*
Previously published in the Winter 2020/21 Issue of Devour: Art & Lit
Canada.

Sights and Sounds at Lake Renaud – *p. 26*
Previously published in the Winter 2019/20 Issue of Tower Poetry.

The Sky Is Full of Shining Stars – *p. 28*
Previously published in Vol. 28, Issue 1 of Montréal Serai.

Landscape of Abandonment – *p. 31*
Previously published in Vol. 33, Issue 4 of Montréal Serai.

White November – *p. 32*
Previously published in the Summer 2019 Issue of Tower Poetry.

This, My Winter – *p. 33*
Previously published in the Summer 2007 Issue of Tower Poetry.

Out Here in the Cottage Country – *p. 35*
Previously published in the Summer 2020 Issue of Tower Poetry.

Sunrise at Marea del Portillo – *p. 37*
A variation of this poem was previously published in the Summer 2021
Issue of Tower Poetry.

Trees in the Winter – *p. 38*
Previously published in the Winter 2020/21 Issue of Tower Poetry.

On This First Warm Day of March – *p. 41*
Previously published in the Summer 2022 Issue of Tower Poetry.

Spring Rain – *p. 42*
Previously published in the Winter 2022/23 Issue of Devour: Art & Lit
Canada.

Cosmic Carousel – *p. 43*
Previously published in the Winter 2022/23 Issue of Tower Poetry.

Kayaking in May – *p. 45*
Previously published in the Summer 2021 Issue of Devour: Art & Lit
Canada.

In My Dream – *p. 46*
Previously published in the Winter 2008/09 Issue of Tower Poetry.

Watching the Sunset on Bar Harbor – *p. 47*
Previously published in Vol. 27, Issue 4 of Montréal Serai.

All That Green – *p. 49*
Previously published in the Winter 2014/15 Issue of Tower Poetry.

Shades of Green – *p. 51*
Previously published in the Winter 2009/10 Issue of Tower Poetry.

Stars over Lake O'Neil – *p. 52*
Previously published in the Summer 2018 Issue of Tower Poetry.

The Shared Path – *p. 53*
Previously published in the Summer 2013 Issue of Tower Poetry.

Reflection – *p. 55*
Previously published in Vol. 28, Issue 1 of Montréal Serai.

In the Early Morning – *p. 56*
Previously published in the Summer 2009 Issue of Tower Poetry.

Lake O'Neil in August – *p. 57*
Previously published in the Summer 2017 Issue of Tower Poetry.

Autumn Leaves – *p. 59*
Previously published in Vol. 27, Issue 4 of Montréal Serai.

Sunday Coffee – *p. 60*
Previously published in the Winter 2012/13 Issue of Tower Poetry.

Cold Winter Morning – *p. 62*
Previously published in the Winter 2015/16 Issue of Tower Poetry.

Frigid December – *p. 63*
Previously published in the Winter 2018/19 Issue of Tower Poetry.

Cold Spring – *p. 65*
Previously published in the Summer 2022 Issue of Devour: Art & Lit Canada.

Raindrops – *p. 66*
Previously published in the Summer 2016 Issue of Tower Poetry.

As the Morning Grows – *p. 67*
Previously published in the Winter 2016/17 Issue of Tower Poetry.

Evening – *p. 69*
Previously published in Vol. 31, Issue 4 of Montréal Serai.

Outside My Bedroom Window – *p. 70*
Previously published in the Summer 2015 Issue of Tower Poetry.

Time – *p. 71*
Previously published in the Winter 2010/11 Issue of Tower Poetry.

Colours of Grey – *p. 72*
Previously published in the Summer 2008 Issue of Tower Poetry.

The Winter Night – *p. 73*
Previously published in the Winter 2017/18 Issue of Tower Poetry.

Her Wish – *p. 74*
Previously published in the Summer 2012 Issue of Tower Poetry.

www.ingramcontent.com/pod-product-compliance
Lightning Source LLC
Chambersburg PA
CBHW051229120626
46547CB00013B/1576